GOD SAID

THIS WILL BE

BRIGHT

God is Love

TYON GIERNET

This publication contains the opinions and ideas of its author. It is intended to provide helpful and informative material on the subjects addressed in the publication. The author and publisher specifically disclaim all responsibility for any liability, loss, or risk, personal or otherwise, which is incurred as a consequence, directly or indirectly, of the use and application of any of the contents of this book.

WRITERS REPUBLIC L.L.C.
515 Summit Ave. Unit R1
Union City, NJ 07087, USA

Website: *www.writersrepublic.com*
Hotline: *1-877-656-6838*
Email: *info@writersrepublic.com*

Ordering Information:
Quantity sales. Special discounts are available on quantity purchases by corporations, associations, and others. For details, contact the publisher at the address above.

Library of Congress Control Number:		2022923477	
ISBN-13:	979-8-88810-212-1	[Paperback Edition]	
	979-8-88810-213-8	[Hardback Edition]	
	979-8-88810-214-5	[Digital Edition]	

Rev. date: 12/14/2022

I'd like to start by saying that the decisions you make in life do not determine who *you* are. You are loved and accepted through all of your imperfections. God is compassionate. From the day you are born, your life is made up of choices. You are born to create, so you create your life and future based on the decisions you make. Your future is in your own hands. Mother earth is filled with billions of souls all trying to make it to heaven. It is up to you to trust your gut and stick to your morals to decipher between good and evil, or darkness and light. Once you are fully open to change, you learn to put yourself first. Unconditional love for yourself gives you the gift to see the real you, only then will you be able to live a life of compassion. A life of unconditional love is what pleases God. God is love.

My first experience with death happened while I was living in Big Lake, Minnesota. I was in fourth grade. I loved it there. I lived in a suburb area that had a plenty of kids to make friends with. I had a best friend named Nolan. I could catch salamanders in the window wells, and my dad even built a tree house! I got my first girlfriend there. Her name was Cora. She would tell me to tie my shoes as tight as I could, and she could always get it untied! I gave her the toy lizard my dad made me, and she held my hand every day after. Some of the kids thought I was the kid from *Stuart Little*, and it made me fit in. I was even asked for an autograph.

That's when tragedy hit my family. My grandpa John died in an accident. He had fallen asleep at the wheel and veered off a bridge. I remember this day like it was yesterday. My family was on the way to see my aunt and uncle when we got the call. We turned the car around, and I asked what we were doing. They said we were heading to my grandparents. I wasn't told why, but I knew that was when my parents found out. I saw my mom crying for the first time during the funeral. I'm tearing up right now thinking about it. I didn't really understand what was happening, but I could feel the sadness. We would sometimes visit the bridge. All I could see was the photo of the truck upside down and lying along the rocks and running water.

After that, we decided to move in with my grandma. It wasn't bad. I got to spend a lot more time outside, and she has this huge mulberry tree! I would use my imagination to create a world in the woods and build huts. I had an imaginary friend that would come with me and I could talk about things like a big brother. The one bad thing was that I would get ticks, and I was deathly afraid of them. I would get nightmares that they were all over the bed, and even with my eyes open, I could still see them. Then even after you realize you're okay, you still feel them crawling on your skin. I bet you can feel an itch just thinking about it right now.

I also remember one day, while waiting for the bus one morning, one of my grandma's dogs, Rex, started for the bus as it was coming down the road. The bus ended up running him over, and I saw the poor thing got hit and rolled underneath, bouncing as it hit the back tire. He got up and went to the ditch. I ran to the bus driver to yell at him, but he just opened the door and said it was the dog's fault. What a terrible thing to say to a kid, you know.

—⟶ℳ⟵—

Some time went by, and I was now about fourteen. We moved out of my grandmas place and moved back to my hometown of Redwood Falls. That's when I think I started to see the world in a different light. I was thinking more like a teenager. I was a good kid who just wanted to have privacy.

My parents got me my first cell phone for Christmas. It was the original Motorola razor. It was dark blue. We had a rule at the house that we would have to turn in our phones at night so we wouldn't be up all night texting people, which is perfectly understandable. I might start doing it for myself now that I think about it. Anyways, it must of been impossible to resist going through my messages and pictures because I was a growing teen. It didn't make it okay though. I would have personal thoughts that I shared with my friends. After being exposed, they punished me by taking away that connection. I felt it was unfair and I lost some trust. That was when I started wanting to rebel, and I entered the emo stage. I started to get bullied at school as well. I would wear skinny jeans and had black hair. I would draw tattoos on my arms and had even tried to cut a star into my hand with a razor and filled it with ink. Luckily, I didn't get an infection. I never felt like I could talk to my parents about things, so I kept everything to myself.

I had just turned fifteen and was a freshman. There was a gay guy back in middle school that would always scope me out and push me over and laugh at me with the friends he was with. He started rumors that I was gay, and it made the rounds at school. It probably didn't help that a girl offered a blowjob if I kissed my guy friend, which we both agreed was a good deal. I was on the football team, wrestling team, track team, and soccer team so that made me feel so awkward in the locker room. I didn't want my classmates to think I was checking them out. Even worse, I didn't know who believed the rumors or not. It was mental hell. Someone being gay didn't bother me. I think everyone has a choice to accept love however they see fit.

I started dating this girl. She was two years older than me. That's when I started to sneak out of the house. There is something about walking through town when there was no vehicle or person to be seen. It gives you the feeling like you are the last person on earth and there's nobody stopping you from doing whatever it is you want to do. It became addicting. I wouldn't even go far; I'd just be a block away, or even sitting in the parking lot outside. Well, this girl and I started to meet up, and my parents found out I'm sneaking out, so I was put on lockdown.

The night I was going to lose my virginity I snuck the girl into the house, and we got down to our underwear when my mom came charging in, yelling my name. It's hilarious thinking about it now. The even better part was, after I was caught, my parents put a security system on the doors so an alarm would trip if I tried to open it. The building also had a fire escape, so I used that a couple times till one time when I forgot to put the screen back in and got caught. They used silicone to seal up the window, so it wouldn't open. Me being the smart and creative type found a way to stick a magnet in the trigger mechanism on the door so the alarm wouldn't go off and I would walked freely. I think they gave up then on how to keep me in after that.

That summer I lost my virginity. It was the most awkward experience I have ever experienced. The day started with me and a buddy riding around town on our bikes, then we went over to his girlfriend's house. His girl and my girl were friends, so it worked out well to be able to see my girlfriend since my parents didn't want me around her. My buddy gave me a condom and said that I should try it today. We all ended up going over to my friend's grandparents place since we would be alone there. We were all upstairs watching a movie when my girlfriend asked me if I wanted to go into the room. I believe it was my buddy's grandparents' bedroom, but I didn't care, I was about to get laid. We got undressed, and I got wrapped up. I had absolutely no idea what I was doing, so I just lay down. I think I got it for a minute, and all the sudden, my buddy was yelling that his grandparents were here! So I jumped up and threw my clothes on. I forgot I still had the condom on. I forgot the time, and I realized I was going to be late for church softball. I jumped on my bike and pedaled to the field. I was in so much pain. The blue balls set in as soon as I hit the outfield, and I realized I was still wrapped up. Now, for anyone that had a similar story, you are not alone, and you will laugh at yourself later. As for me, I held on to the fact that I did something I shouldn't have. And it wasn't really special like I would've wanted it to be. I was also way too young to be messing around like that. Being an adult now, I think we should change the way we think about sex. It's a spiritual thing; however, many see it is a physical experience that results in a pregnancy or sometimes an STD, but it's so much more than that. Maybe the talk about the birds and the bees should be told in a way that connects to nature and that procreation serves a divine purpose.

Everything that makes you, you and everything that makes the other person them is interlaced in the creation of a new life. All the emotions and undealt-with trauma we carry at the moment of conception are then passed down into the new life. That baby will then have all of what makes both parents spiritually. They grow up deciphering good and bad based on the traits they were born with. That is why it is so important to find your soulmate. The only way to find your soulmate is if you love yourself unconditionally. A child born from soulmates gives the life you helped create a better opportunity to create more good in the world.

While hanging out with that girl, I tried smoking weed for the first time. I got picked up before school, and in the car that picks me up were some schoolmates that were a little older than me. They asked me if I ever tried it, and I said no. Well, in their eyes, it must have been a perfect opportunity to get me high, so we hit the McDonald's drive-through. I got some of those cinnamon rolls, but my problem was I could not for the life of me get the box to close. It was the funniest thing ever. So it became an inside joke.

We showed up at school, and the high was in full effect. I had to go to class, and my buddy had the same class as me. We actually sat facing each other in the room but were on opposite sides. During the reading time, when it was dead silent, I looked up and met my friend's gaze. I couldn't control it and burst out laughing. That was the first time I had ever had to go to the office. I had never made a mistake at school, and when I walked out, I still couldn't stop laughing. I was laughing because I couldn't believe that my first time getting kick out of class was because I was laughing.

After that, I knew that marijuana wasn't what I thought it would be. It seemed scary before I tried it, but after trying it, I saw all the benefits from using it. It helps lift your spirits. It also helps with creativity. Research shows that it has all of these health benefits. I just couldn't wrap my head around why a plant that does so much good and is naturally growing on God's green earth could be looked at so negatively and be illegal.

When I was sixteen, I had my first experience with a suicide. Jordan was good friends with one of my cousins, and I was good friends with Jordan's sister. I remember my cousin calling me and told me what happened. I was in shock. I didn't really know what to think at the time, but I ran to my mom and told her that Jordan died and that I needed to go over to talk with my cousins. I got over there as fast as I could, and we ended up going over to Jordan's house. It was a very depressing scene. When we walked in the house, there was a heavy feeling. There were so many people there, but we were all supporting each other.

It only got worse after that. A week later, another suicide happened. Brad was in my homeroom class. He looked like a young Tom Cruise. He was the rebel type and was quiet but good with the girls.

Those suicides hit me hard. The whole town seemed to be depressed. There was this dark cloud over the town. It didn't help that Thanksgiving was just a few days away. Now every year we will be reminded. We started group counseling at school. It ended up just being a place to cry with friends and family. As the year went on, the numbers went up. There were accidents and suicides every few months. Nobody knew how to handle all of that.

The positive thing that came out of that was the sense of community. During a time of tragedy and confusion, the one thing we all naturally do is try to comfort each other. People started to care more about one another. Groups were formed, and even the school started to create an awareness. I'm sure the staff at school got an update on how to deal with some of the emotions displayed by the students. Because these happened around Thanksgiving, it made us realize that there are a million things we take for granted, and it gave us something to be thankful for.

I started to cut myself during that year. The cutting became kind of addicting. The sharp scratch followed by drips of warm blood felt like I was releasing some of the sadness. Feeling anything felt good as I was so numb to the world.

I was severely depressed and suicidal. I also was on medication. I hated the feeling that I had to depend of meds in order to feel happy. That didn't sit right with me. One night I got the idea that I would sneak out during the night and drive to the family cabin to end my life. I knew my dad had a shotgun there, so I got a couple things packed and waited till it was late in the night. I walked out my bedroom door quietly but was met by my mom. She was sleeping, but I must have woken her up. She asked me what I was doing, so I came up with an excuse. I went back to my room, and I thought I would have to ditch school instead.

The next day I dropped my sisters off at school and drove off to Willmar, Minnesota. They had a skate park, and I wanted to skate one last time before ending my life. I wasted some time with a Sharpie drawing on the grip tape, wanting to leave a little art behind. After that I decided to come to Green Lake Bible Camp to see if God really existed and if he could stop me. I walked around for a bit, talking to God as if it was all his fault. I went to the cabin where I first got to stay and rang the dinner bell. I got nothing. I was walking back to my car when I noticed a little paper heart that said, "God loves you" at the back. I laughed a little and thought, *Well, it is a Bible camp. So this doesn't mean much.* I kept it though. I put it in my car and drove to the cabin to do the deed.

I was sitting on the dock trying to work up the guts to do it when one of my grandma's old friends came, shouting and screaming, "I found him." I guess the cops and all my friends and family were looking for me.

I was then put in a mental ward and stripped of all my possessions. I can't even bring my guitar in, which was a crutch for me. I felt completely alone and in a prison while being in a prison of my mind. I was placed in the worst possible situation. A mental ward is where you are stripped of everything that makes you human: no shoes because you might take the string and kill yourself, no locks on the doors, the shower has no door, your room is a jail cell. You're given medicine every morning and night, then your then put into groups of other people like yourself. You have to open up or you won't get out of the hospital. I have faked my way out of three different hospitals, which made me a pretty good actor. I can put a face on faster than you can blink. It's sad really. I know I'm not the only one.

I got a funny story about one of these places. When I was going through the intake process, I noticed a good-looking girl that would be staying in the same pod area as me. We ended up being able to be alone for a while in the art recreation area one night and got to talking. We started to flirt a bit and left it at that. The next day we found out there weren't any cameras in the back section of the room. So we sat down on the floor behind the counter and made out for a while before being caught. I never did get her name. But that just goes to show you the system doesn't care much.

The positive thing was that you learn that there are others that go through things that they can't handle too. Age, race, religion, background, or any of that doesn't matter. You see it all. I also got a close look at the various disorders as well. It opens your eyes to how people are affected by things you would think are simple.

—m—

After I got out, I went back to high school, a junior. I was now on medication and counseling. I ended up seeing multiple counsellors. I never got the chance to choose one. They were offered to me according to my preference of a male or a female. Like what kind of crap is that? Then as a teen, how are you supposed to trust anyone that can easily talk to my parents. The first guy I had, I didn't see more than once. The room was filled with baby toys because he worked with kids. It made me feel like I wasn't going to be taken seriously.

This was around the time when some bullying started to happen again, but it wasn't the gay guy. The rumors never went away, and now I have nothing to lose, so I started to stick up for myself and anyone else who was getting bullied. That was when I really started to cheer for the underdogs. I made friends with all the different cliques until I was involved in a big argument that made me feel unsafe at school. A friend of mine from back when I was sneaking out was getting made fun of. The guy said he could kick his ass. So I told the guy if he did anything to my friend, I would curb stomp him. He decided to make it known that everyone thinks I'm gay and I should just quit hiding it. We had a little stare down, and other choice words were said. So I transferred schools. I deserved a new start.

I would spend my summers working for my dad at the business he took over. It started out just moving the lawn till he taught me how to cut glass. I didn't mind the job at first, but like any other kid during summer, I would rather be doing something else. I got a job being a lifeguard. There was this girl that was catfishing me and a couple other guys I knew. I've never seen or spoke with the girl in person, but she found me and took pictures of me at work. She said I was a cute lifeguard and such, so I started to talk to her every night. Eventually, we would have phone sex. Then things started to get dark very fast. She turned really controlling. One time, I told her I cut, and she wanted proof. She told me that the cut wasn't that bad and that I should make it worse. So I did. You can still see the scar to this day. I cut my ties with her, but it still haunted me for a while.

I was now going to be attending New London-Spicer High School. One of my old buddies had moved and was going to school there. My parents had a cabin on Norway Lake where I had made some friends from the area, so I thought this would be the new start that I needed. Unfortunately, my friend and I hadn't talked for years and we had changed so much that we didn't really stay as friends.

I loved that school. I was getting along with everyone pretty well, and I knew some girls from the area, so I wasn't completely alone. The cool part about that school was that they had a rule where if you wanted to wear a hat during the day, you would go put a quarter in a jar in the front office. They used the money for things at the school. One class I wish I knew they had was astrology. They also had German language class.

My first day in German class I noticed a girl by the name of Halee. She was gorgeous! I worked up the courage to sit by her. She was super friendly and smelled like perfume every day. We would write little flirty things on each other's homework, and when we had to get in groups, we would always pick each other. We started to hang out after school and I was thankful for our friendship. She was such a loving person and made me feel welcomed. She would hug strangers and just make everyone's day.

The driving back and forth from Redwood and New London got tiring, and winter made it worse, so I decided to switch back to Redwood Valley. It was my senior year. When I got back, it felt like I didn't belong, but I tried my best.

When spring came around, I got some bad news. I was sitting in my science class when my phone started to buzz. I asked to go to the bathroom so I can answer it. It was one of my friends from New London, and she gave me the news that Halee committed suicide. I asked her what she knew about it, and I was told she was getting bullied. A senior wanted to take her to prom, and the girls were jealous. I'm not sure if that's true or not. I'll never know. Anyways, now I am sobbing in the hallway, and I have nobody to seek comfort from. I called my mom to ask if I could come home for the day, and she let me. She asked what was wrong, and I told her that one of my friends had committed suicide. The response I got wasn't expected. She asked, "Were you good friends with her?" She didn't know the extent of the relationship I had with her, and I didn't want to tell her because I didn't want her to know. I didn't trust telling my parents much since I felt like I would get into trouble. Also, I just didn't want them in my personal life among my social life. I chose to deal with that one in silence.

I turned eighteen that summer, and that was when I started to snowball down the wrong path. I started to not really give a shit. I was working for my dad, and he had this pop machine that I would break into and steal the money for weed or cash to walk around with. I would cut myself to get out of work. I would steal from the till at work. I was surprised my parents haven't killed me yet, and it was only getting worse.

I picked up the habit of smoking and drinking. I was even smoking that fake weed they call k2. Surprisingly, you could buy it at the gas station. I was smoking in the house and would always lie about it. They found my stash, but I told them it was k2 from the gas station and it was legal, so they can't say I can't smoke it as I was eighteen.

One of my friends had a job as a blackjack dealer. He figured out a way to cheat and taught me. I would go out to the casino with twenty bucks and walk out with amounts ranging from one hundred to eight hundred. We eventually got caught, and luckily, we didn't get any jail time, just banned for life. That wasn't the worst way possible to get money. I started to hang out with the wrong crowd. I even started hanging out with the guy I was about got into a fight with at school. My girlfriend at the time probably hated me. We had just moved into a house, but I decided to treat her like crap. I was cheating and letting people move in who wouldn't pay rent. I think I even dumped her.

The house turned into a trap house, and if you don't know what that is, it's a place to sell and use drugs and party. That's when I was first exposed to heroin and meth. I didn't participate, but I watched what it can do to people. One time I remember one of the guys broke off some sheet rock, wrapped it up, and sold it to a dude. The dude came back and wanted more, which blew my mind. Addiction was a real thing, like holy. I was between jobs, and nobody was paying, so I had to ask my dad if I could work for him again.

To make matters worse, we started to rob people for weed and cash. The crew I was hanging out with decided to hold a guy at gunpoint at a deal. We took his stash and his money, and even the radio to his truck.

One night I would never forget was when we headed to a party in Minneapolis. I didn't know anyone but my roommate and one other friend. We get there, and it was a legit house party. I had never been to one like this. They had wristbands and a bartender. It was a Halloween party, and it was around midnight when the owner shut it down. We didn't want to stop partying, so we hopped into a random person's trunk and went to the after party. At this point, I don't even have a shirt on, but I didn't care where it went. We stopped and got into this party, but there was an argument going on outside between two groups. Everyone was now out on the street getting ready to watch this huge fight that was breaking out. It did, and it got bad very quick. A couple guys jumped into a car and drove straight toward the fight. They only hit one guy, but as that guy tried to get up, someone hit him in the head with a bottle and then again. This time the bottle broke and split his face halfway off. The car then headed down to the end of the street and turned around and hit him again. I couldn't watch anymore, so I started walking away from the situation. That was when the police arrived. We all scattered. The guys I came with found me, and we have no way back to the car we came in. So we had to walk all the way across the city to the house where the car was. Mind you, I'm a 125-pound White kid walking shirtless that has no business in these parts. We got to the car, and we didn't have the keys. I was now the lucky one that must convince the girl I treated like dirt to come get us. Thankfully, she did. My inconsiderate ass didn't bother to drive back.

Eventually, I got out of that place. I'm twenty now, and I moved back home because I can't afford to pay the rent by myself. I worked for my dad for a bit longer, but during my time at the shop, things started to get dark in my life again. I fell into a depression working nine to five. All my friends live an hour away. I couldn't make enough money to go and get my own place, and I had no clue where I would work. I started to cut myself again. This time it was to be able to leave work and get stitches. I just wanted to have the day off, but I felt guilty to ask for a personal day because I've had this fake face on for a while, and they were proud of my progress.

I finally got my parents to let me stay in the cabin, and I got a job at Rue 21, a clothing store. I made a ton of friends and started to throw parties at the cabin. Now these were like big parties. If there wasn't one at the cabin, I would find one. There was always one happening. I was starting to have the worst hangovers, and I was starting to feel drained. I got the bright idea to cut myself at work again so I could leave. My parents found out from the neighbors about the parties, but I just shrugged it off and continued to disobey them. Eventually, they told me I was no longer allowed to be there. They locked the place up, but I would break in sometimes and have little parties with a couple friends.

I got an apartment at a place called Willow Run in Willmar, Minnesota. My parents wanted me out so bad that they helped me get it. This was a bad apartment complex at the time, full of gangs and drug dealers. Again, I let some friends move in with me. We called the apartment the Tipi. It became a popular spot because all my friends were younger than me and were still living with their parents. They called me Chief, and we all had our names. When we would have get-togethers, we would drink and smoke. We would also have like potlucks, and I felt like I was caring for them, giving them a space to be themselves.

But eventually, it started to get toxic. I let a guy move in that I wasn't really friends with, but he had the supply for weed, so it was nice. He eventually got the hots for my girlfriend, and they ended up sleeping together on my bed on New Year's when I was at the casino with a friend. I found out there was a party at my apartment, so I asked to talk with my girlfriend to ask why everyone was there. I found she was in my room with the guy I let move in, and it really hurt because I felt I was helping everyone, and instead, I was being used to the max. I held my ground though, and when I got back, there was hell to pay.

I got into my first fight when I got back. I was working when a Facebook post turned into an argument. I was tired of hearing the talk because I'm terrible with comebacks. That just made me angrier. I told the guy I'll meet him at the cabin when I get off from work. The nerve of that girl though. She drove him to the cabin to watch it go down. It was winter at the time, and when they showed up, they had a group to watch. I had a couple friends with me. I told them if anyone jumps in, I expect some help. Well, it was time to face the guy. I'm a 130-pound guy and athletic, and he is like 170 and was in the army. I took off my jacket, and he wanted to do the whole face-to-face thing. He told me so swing first. I didn't say anything, and I didn't hesitate. I missed, and he got behind my back and punched me two times right where your head meets your neck. Boy, that sent me in a rage. I flipped him over my back. He landed on his back, and I jumped on his chest. I got two hits in before he grabbed my wrists. I was trying to get my hands back, and he was mocking me, saying, "Pick me up!" I kind of laughed and called him fat. I couldn't free my hands, so I got the bright idea to headbutt him. I pulled my head back and pulled my arms open, forcing my head right into his nose and teeth, which gave me a nasty cut on my head. His arms went up, and I got another couple hits in before he rolled over.

We were wrestling a bit, and he freaking bit my arm. I dropped, and he got on top of me. Luckily, I knew some MMA moves and got him in a choke hold. He asked me if I was done, so I let him go. We got up, and his friend wanted a piece of me as well, but I flicked him off and told them to leave. Anytime I thought about that night, my adrenalin would kick in.

Before I left that apartment, we all had tried multiple drugs: shrooms, pills, huffed air duster, and taken more than prescribed amounts of cough and cold medicine. Then there was the usual weed and hard liquor. I got a DWI in February that year. I was drinking with friends and had just snorted a cap full of tequila. Don't ask why because I honestly don't know. I had just traded my car for a Pontiac Fiero, a little sports car. My friend wanted to get a pack of cigs, and I wanted to show him the new whip. We got in the car, and as I was turning the corner, I laid it down a bit, sending us in a drift around the corner. I didn't notice there was a cop sitting right there when it happened. He followed me to the gas station where he pulled me over. He asked if I had been drinking and twenty-year-old me said, "Nope!" I had to do the tests anyway and got locked up for a few hours.

The next day I was packing and getting everything out of the apartment so I could move back home. I moved back in. I was still drinking heavily, and in a week, I got my second DWI. This time it was a little worse. I had been drinking most of the night, and I wanted to talk to an ex. She had a boyfriend at the time that I was jealous of. I convinced myself while drunk that she was cheating on me. I got the nerve to walk a few blocks and try to start a fight. I couldn't get in, so I ripped off the guy's mirror to his truck and went home. The drinking continued, and the cops stopped by to warn me that if I left the house again, they would arrest me. Well, that didn't stop me. I drove over, and before I could get to the door, the cop lights came on. I was arrested again. When I got out the next morning, it was Thanksgiving. I had been in such bad shape when I got out that my body went into this full body cramp and I couldn't breathe. My dad carried me to the car, and we went to the hospital. I got some medication. I calmed down and was sent on my way.

I am twenty-one now and on probation. I only had to stay in jail four days. I didn't get to have a twenty-first celebration at the bar, but I did celebrate with my family. I started to work full time for my dad. I got my act together finally and felt good about life. I started to see a girl, and I really liked her. We had an on-and-off relationship toward the end of my senior year that led into that summer. I didn't treat her very well the first time around. I had cheated on her a few times. This time I was on my feet. That was until this girl I was dating got narcissistic. I was clueless, but my parents could see what she was doing. We were living together in my parents' place, and they wanted her to move out. That didn't sit well with me, so we ended up getting into some heated arguments. I was stuck. I had to choose between this girl I loved and my family. She never moved out, and she found someone else at the same time. Little to my knowledge, she was full-on dating him and just living with me, using me. I felt so guilty for verbally abusing my parents and causing them extreme heartbreak. I couldn't help myself, I should have listened to my gut, but instead, I started to drink. I dumped the girl and apologized to my parents. They were very understanding. I still felt bad for all the ugly things I said.

I didn't quite have my license back, so I ended up having to ride a bike to the liquor store. Every time I got on that bike, I felt shame because the reason I was riding this thing was because of the drinking, and now I was using it to get more alcohol. The one good thing about using the bike was I found a new hobby. I started to ride bike around town catching Pokémon and picked up a fishing habit. It kept me out of a depression of sorts. I just had addiction now that I couldn't kick.

I got off probation early for good behavior, and the fines were paid off with the help of my parents. After two years, I got my license back, and the first place I wanted to go was back up to Willmar.

Things were good for a couple years, and that's when I moved into a house with my best friend since high school. Our relationship was on and off, but we would always end up being friends again.

I was twenty-four now and at the Hawaii house. We lived on Hawaii Avenue. I was finally on my own again and off probation, so it was time to live it up again. I started to drink more and got a nasty Adderall habit. I met a girl, and she loved Jack Daniels just as much as me. We would have competitions on who could outdrink each other. One night I had drank most of the bottle, and the hangover was terrible. I was vomiting every twenty minutes and hardly could keep water down. I knew I had to quit and ended up slowing down to drinking on the weekends. I also ended things with her and was back out on the prowl.

That was when I met my future wife. We started talking, and I really liked her. She is beautiful and outgoing. We would sit out on the porch and talk all night. She liked my friends, and we knew of each other. She had dated someone that was in the friend group that I didn't really talk much. One night before I asked her to date me, there was a guy trying to rekindle an old flame. I put a stop to it by asking her to be my girl that night.

A few weeks went by, and I asked her if she wanted to move in with me, and she did. We were doing great, and I cut down the drinking to only when we had friends over. I went upstairs to my room one night while we had friends over. She had her phone charging, and I saw the screen light up. I looked over at it and saw it was her ex. I opened the messages. She was telling him that she missed him and what they had. I felt so betrayed, and I brought it up later. She talked me into forgiving her, so I forgave her. It was early in the relationship, so I gave her the benefit of the doubt.

A few months went by, and things were great. My family was taking a trip to Mexico, and that was when I cheated on her. I was talking on the phone with an old friend that lived in Mexico. We talked all night, and I was drinking beer mixed with hard liquor. We started to talk about a time a long time ago when we first met. It was at a church event, and we snuck out to make out. We are a lot older now, so we got to talking about our bodies and sent some pictures back and forth. I saved them and forgot about it. I felt terrible and even told the girl the next day that I wasn't in the right mind and that I love my girlfriend and that I was sorry for convincing her to send pictures. I felt so guilty that I bought my girlfriend a promise ring. I knew I never would do that to her again.

I went home, and it was almost my birthday, so she had gifts waiting for me. I gave her the ring. I had forgotten that I had placed the pictures in a locked app. The app had pictures from other girlfriends in it. She found the pictures a few days later when she went through my phone. I admitted what I did and told her that I made sure that the girl knew I wasn't in the right mind and stuff. The ring didn't really mean much anymore but, She forgave me, and we were a happy couple for a year.

During that year, we took acid. I didn't like it much because when we took it, my girlfriend would be with another guy all night. I told her how much it bothered me and especially since when we are on acid, my acid experience would be bad.

I got back into my drinking habit, but I didn't want my girlfriend to know, so I would sneak drinks between times going to the bathroom, or I would hide a bottle outside so when I would go smoke a cigarette, I could take a chug.

I would say this was the part where I started to hide my drinking from everyone. I would feel ashamed of taking shots in the morning and throughout the day, but I couldn't control it anymore. It started to become so automatic. My girlfriend and I wanted to move out of my buddy's house. It was small and not always the cleanest. My parents found a house that was under foreclosure out on West Norway Lake behind a horse ranch. I told them that we wanted it, and we worked out a deal to pay the rent and whatnot if they provided it for us. I was so happy when we got the place. It was absolutely gorgeous! It's an old brick house with ivy vines growing up the one corner on 3.5 acers of grassy land. There are huge old oak trees with a pine tree border next to a cornfield that extends with rolling hills and a creek. At the end of the field is a lake.

Being twenty-five and having a place to call our own really made this relationship feel like it was going to be our last. I was still hiding my drinking and was putting down a pint of vodka a day.

We got on the summer softball league that she had played on for years. I don't know how, but I played pretty good with a buzz. I did trip a few times, but nobody noticed. In between innings, I would run to the porta potty and take a shot. I always would bring those little individual shots.

Halfway through the season, my girlfriend told me she had a brother that I didn't know about. She told me that her parents adopted him a while back and he was a little older, meaning I wouldn't have met him. One night, she then told me she was going to go see him that night. They were going to watch a movie and catch up.

Hours later, it was getting late, and I was wondering where she was. I asked her, but there was no reply. Three o'clock in the morning rolled around, and she texted me saying she fell asleep and had drank a little, so she was going to stay the night. I was clearly skeptical. When she got back home, I asked a million questions. She denied anything fishy was going on, and I felt like maybe I was just being insecure.

A week or so went by, and I got a message from the wife of one of the guys that plays against us at softball. I learned that on that night she was at her brother's place, she was actually with this other guy. I was heartbroken and knew that my gut feeling was right all along. And she had been lying to me for days because I hadn't stop asking if it was true. Eventually, I contacted the guy, and he admitted to everything. I then showed her the messages from the guy, and she broke down. But she said not all of that was true. Well, eventually, she talked me into forgiving her. She said she was still heartbroken over what happened when I was in Mexico. She forgave me, so I decided to forgive her.

We were still friends with the crew from Willmar, and we decided to try acid again. I gave in and took some. I was hoping that this time she would have listened, but nope, she was all over that guy from the last time she was tripping. This time it was worse. She was lying on the bed with him right in front of me for hours. I couldn't sleep, and I didn't want to be there anymore, so I told her to get up, that we were leaving. My drinking started to get worse. I was feeling like nothing I said was getting across. I don't want to upset her because she would tell me that he was like a brother to her, that he has always been there for her, even before me, so she wasn't going to stop being friends with him. I said, "Fine."

We tried molly next, otherwise known as the ecstasy drug. This time we weren't in a room full of guys. There were a couple of girls, and one of them I had a thing with years ago. It was going to be awkward. I was still upset about the time on acid and felt like I could open up a bit with the help of the drug. We started to draw on each other. I pissed of my girlfriend by letting a girl write her name along my pant line. I thought nothing of it because carefree is the feeling you get from molly.

My girlfriend was working at my dad's business in Spicer with me. Every day she would write me notes. It was cute, and I looked forward to them so much. That was until I was cleaning the bathroom and saw under her clothes a note written for the guy she was always cuddling with. It described in detail exactly what she wanted to do with him. My heart sunk and instant chaos in my mind. She convinced me she wrote it for her friend that wanted to be with him, so I kind of brushed it off. I knew I was never going to get her to admit it. To this day I still don't have a solid answer to how the note got there.

—⁙—

I was now twenty-six, and my drinking was at a half liter of vodka a day. We had a good spell for a while, but my drinking was becoming obvious. She found my stash and all the places I would hide the liquor. I felt so ashamed. I kept this lie from her and everyone else for so long, and now she knew. She also had been going through my phone and found out that I had been watching porn. She told me I had to quit drinking and watching porn or she was leaving me. I seriously tried, but every time I would, I'd start to get withdrawals from the alcohol. It was so hard to quit. I couldn't. The porn, on the other hand, was giving me the intimacy I was asking for. That became a big problem as well. It got just as addicting as the drinking. I got better at hiding both. I even started to put my bottles in the ceiling so she wouldn't find them.

One thing I never did was go through her phone. I never got the chance. I don't think I wanted to know what I would find either. She would tell me the password, and I would forget it within minutes. Now my memory had started to get pretty bad that I wouldn't be able to remember what I did just two days ago. I would forget so many things and it was incredibly embarrassing.

19

We had been on a good spell for few months, and I was actually thinking about marrying her. I cut down the drinking to only a pint every other day. So I felt basically sober. I was still hooked on porn, but my excuse was because we never got intimate anymore. It was true, but it was still disrespectful. I got caught again because she went through my Internet history. I couldn't get away with anything on my phone. She would check my emails, snaps, texts, deleted history, and even my cloud space. She was going to leave, but I begged her to stay. She said, "Fine, this is the last time." I was grateful she didn't leave.

We had a rocky relationship but we honestly loved each other. We would go to EDM shows and take trips to duluth. We were really good at board games and laughed a lot. We would challenge each other to little things and I loved to come home to her. I didn't want to lose all of that.

A couple weeks went by, and we started to talk about rings and what kind she wanted and what shape it would be. I took notes and talked to some jewelers. I was excited, so I told my parents about it. They seemed happy for me and was all for it. My girlfriend was telling me how amazing it would be if she gets a proposal before her birthday. Well, I didn't really have the money to buy a nice ring, but I was getting a bonus at work that month, so I used every penny and more to get a perfect ring she wanted.

When the ring came in, I did what all men should do and spoke with her father before I asked for her hand in marriage. I was so nervous because her dad was the type that when you say something, he would look at you like you're a stupid kind of deal. When I asked, he went, "Oh really," and laughed. But he gave me the go ahead.

So a couple days later, after her sister's birthday, she jumped in the shower. I ran downstairs and arranged the candles in a heart shape and put down some rose petals. Then I told her to come downstairs. I got on one knee and asked her to marry me! I knew I was getting a yes, but I was more excited to show her what I got her. She loved it, and we kissed and hugged. We went upstairs to get ready for bed when she gave me a gift. It was wrapped in wrapping paper and about the size of a highlighter. I opened it, and it was a positive pregnancy test! We were going to have a baby. I was honestly completely overwhelmed. Not only was I going to be telling people that I was engaged, but I was also going to share that I was having a kid!

Now I know why she wanted to be engaged so badly and why wasn't I informed. It was a really big step just to say, "I want to spend the rest of my life with you," let alone us having a kid. I understand why she was scared and I don't blame her.

Things between us got a lot better, but my drinking wasn't getting any better. I still couldn't kick the habits, but nine months later, my little girl was born. I thought for sure that when the baby came, I would have the extra encouragement to get sober. I felt crummy inside because I knew I couldn't last the couple nights in the hospital before having withdrawals. Before I knew it, I was heading out and getting a bottle while getting breakfast for us. At this time, I would only be taking a shot when my hands would get shaky. Being a father, I really, really wanted to quit. How do you quit drinking while keeping it hidden. I have to do it alone. What kind of person chooses the bottle over their kid? Come to find out, you can't. The stress of having a kid plus the pressure of hiding the smell of alcohol were taking a toll on me. Now I was feeling stuck and like I was losing control of my life.

That was when I said, "That's it." I was going to try to slowly work my way down again. It was taking so long to cut down. There were those bad days at work, and I didn't want to deal with having to put my sober face on. It felt impossible. Then I got the bright idea to quit cold turkey. After five days of withdrawals, I finally admitted I wasn't sick from the flu, but I had been drinking so much for so long. I went to the hospital, and I had to stay for two days. I asked my fiance to come visit. I got the feeling she really didn't want to see me. I gave her plenty of reasons not to. She came but didn't bring our kid. So I asked where she was. I was told she was in the car with the acid guy. That broke my heart. My daughter was being cared for by a guy I strongly don't like, and I was sitting in a hospital bed trying to get sober. I knew she was upset and he had always been there for her. It must be pretty rough for her dealing with a newborn and finding out that, yet again, your fiancé was drinking.

In my eyes, I have been battling this problem for so long, and my efforts weren't being received. How could they? Nobody knew.

That was when the drinking got worse. I was starting to take swigs every time I would have to run upstairs. I would chug a bit before I walked in the door after work. I would wake up in the middle of the night and take a drink. One night I will never forget was when it was my turn to get our girl down. I was always a little more patient and could get her down easier. Sometimes I would fall asleep with her on my chest in the rocker. Well, this time I ended up falling asleep with her, and when I woke up, my little girl was still asleep, but she was about to fall off my lap. I felt like the worst person in the world. I knew that it was dark and you're cuddling a little baby, but it was only eight or nine in the evening, and I had been buzzed. After I would get her down, I would always feel like it was okay to drink myself to sleep. My fiancée wouldn't be able to wake me up when our little girl would be crying at night, and she had every right to be pissed off. I had completely lost control of the drinking.

I got sick again from withdrawals. I was trying so hard on my own at this point. I got to work one morning, and I was feeling pretty off. I knew my withdrawal was coming in, and I had to work mobile that day, so I didn't get a chance to get a bottle. I got about three hours into the day, and I started to vomit. The guy I was working with didn't know I had this problem, so I just said I wasn't feeling good. We were on our way to a job site, and I didn't have my seat belt on because my stomach hurt so bad, and of course, we get pulled over. I got a seatbelt ticket. I honestly wanted to puke on the cops shoes because she was all arrogant and I am struggling to sit up straight.

After that I couldn't take it anymore, so I called my dad and said I had to go home sick. When I got to my truck, I had just a little bit of vodka left, so I chugged it. I was hoping I would be able to make it the hour drive home but I threw it up instead. I had no water and nothing to eat. I stopped at the soonest gas station and got a water and a can of chicken broth. I did my best to sip the soup down and get any water I could handle. I had to pull over three times to puke by the time I made it thirty-five miles. Ten minutes from home, my body started to shut down. My whole body started to tighten up. I couldn't breathe, and I couldn't drive any longer. I turned around and headed to my parents' house that was two miles away.

I checked myself into a detox and recovery center that day, but my withdrawals were so bad I had to go to the emergency room. After the hospital stay I went back to the recovery center. The facility reminded me of the mental hospital and a prison. I knew I wasn›t going to like it and checked myself out. The alcohol was finally completely out of my body for the first time in years. I was prescribed some depression and anxiety medication and told I should enter a program. I did try a couple AA groups. The problem I had was that most of the people there were way older than me and had been in the program for years and I was fresh out of the hospital. I was also not the outgoing type, and I had no clue what to say. I listened for a while and then the Bible was brought out. I thought, *They really want a Bible study right now?* How was reading from the Holy Book going to help me? I walked out of that meeting and bought a bottle.

I was finding myself in a depression again, and my attitude toward life was not the greatest. I was starting to feel used at work because I was running the daily work, from scheduling measure ups, ordering windows, unloading trucks, then servicing the windows, sending out bills, and keeping the shop/work van in order. I was thinking suicide might be the only way out of the cycle that I have built.

That was when a new problem started to arise. My fiancée has been wanting to go out more and I didnt have a problem with it. We agreed that she wasn't going to her ex-boyfriend's birthday party, but on the day of the party, she informed me she wanted to go with some friends and that they would only be there for an hour. I caved and told her it was fine and to let me know when she would leave. Well, she stayed all night. At three in the morning, I was calling and texting but no replies. She spent the night there. I came to find out her friends left after an hour and she was all over her ex.

I was now twenty-seven, and it was the year of the wedding. My fiancée and I have been bickering a lot more now. The fights were useless. I have been able to hide the drinking. And, well, now that I've built up a tolerance, it was actually hard to get drunk anymore or at least feel drunk. I was getting to the point where I feel like we were just living together. I was so busy trying to keep my secret hidden and help raise our child that I forgot how to show any affection. I was not cheating on her or anything, but was just in this zombie-like state watching the days go by and dealing with life as it came. I'm starting to create two separate lives for myself and i dont like either one that I'm creating. I can't tell you how badly I want to quit. I tried. I just couldn't admit it at that point. What would people think? I was about to get married and I had a kid. That could all be taken away from me. My job would be on the line because I was driving around every day going to jobs and taking swigs to keep the shakes away. I started to cut again. This time the cuts were gashes. I had to make it look like a work accident you know, so they got deep.

August came, and the wedding was on. We had the ceremony in a greenhouse. It was absolutely gorgeous. At the altar, we had a giant dream catcher, and the place was full of green plants and flowers. That morning I hopped in the truck and set out to town to meet all the groomsmen. It was a pretty good day! I was only drinking a little. I wanted to feel sober for the big day. I did well the whole day. I hardly had a sip. I'd say the only bad part about that day was that the greenhouse was cooking all of us or the fact that I cried when she was walking up the aisle and her dad and my now wife were laughing at me. My best man made fun of me as well. it might be funny to them but to me it was all love and joyful tears. I have never seen my wife look so beautiful and the fact that I get to marry her built up so much I had to let it out. The reception went well. I just wish I could've really enjoyed the big day fully. I couldn't stop thinking about how much I have or haven't drunk. After the dinner, most of my groomsmen were on the hotel room snorting coke and passing around molly. I wasn't aware of that till I walked in on them. I went to the room to take a swig from the bottle that I had hidden in the room.

Our honeymoon was in Jamaica! We had a great time. The weather was perfect the whole time. The pool was huge! They had live music every night. It was an all-inclusive resort. It was full of restaurants and shops. They even had a casino. My wife actually won like eighty bucks the one night on blackjack. I think our favorite restaurant was the Italian place. I'm pretty sure we ate there three or four times. We got to swim with dolphins and saw some of the surrounding area as well. On the way there, I was so nervous about how I was going to feel not being able to drink all day and travel hours to our resort. I was fine until we landed in Jamaica. When going through customs, I couldn't even write my information on the card since my hands were so shaky. I had to get my wife to write it for me. I came up with the excuse that my adrenalin was pumping since we arrived. When we got to the resort three hours later, I guess you could say we had drinks all night, but I had gone and got a little bottle for myself and one to hide. I couldn't help it, I just had to get a stronger buzz since my tolerance was so high.

It was killing me that I had to find a hiding spot for the liquor in our room. I was stressed the whole trip because I was so scared of my wife finding it or the cleaning ladies taking it out. I also ended up buying some weed there. How can you not? It's Jamaica! I didn't really smoke much of it, and it stunk pretty bad. I didn't want to get caught by the staff.

—m—

October came, and my wife and I were going to host a Halloween party like the year before. We had a babysitter, and we got the whole house ready. We invited a bunch of people. Some said they might be able to make it, and some lived far away, so we didn't expect much. Well, we got four people to show up. We then came up with a different plan. We would just go to the bar. When we got there, the group of friends that I don't really like was there. The guy from acid night and my wife's ex-boyfriend were more than friendly with my wife, from what everyone was telling me. The acid guy was all depressed, and the ex-boyfriend invited us over at the bar. So we went there, but I couldn't get my wife to hang around by me. She was busy holding on to her ex-boyfriend's knees and telling him, "Oh no, you aren't that bad looking." That sent me over the edge. I started to drink a little faster. Just watching this all happen made my gut wrench. I grabbed her and pulled her aside and told her we were leaving. Well, that must have pissed her off because things just got worse. She was now crying about it to her ex and all the girls that were asking her. Now I had a dilemma. I was begging my wife to leave with me, and now all of these people were telling me to leave. Obviously, my wife didn't want to go . I had nothing else to do but go sleep in the car. It was a cold October in Minnesota, and I didn't want to be sitting in a car on the road with the car running while intoxicated, so I just huddled up and tried to sleep.

Four o'clock in the morning rolled around, and the party was still going on. I was freezing, so I walked to the back of the house where the fire pit was to warm up and to see if I could see my wife. I saw her, and she was in an embrace with her ex's little brother. I told him to let my wife go and back the fuck up. I was ready to smack the crap out of this seventeen-year-old kid. He told I was controlling, and my wife ran inside. Acid guy was standing right there next to him and saying it was not worth it. I backed off and cooled down. I decided, screw it, she can find her own way home.

The next morning, around 10:00 a.m., I saw a black pickup come rolling up the driveway to our house. Low and behold, the ex-boyfriend was the one she found to bring her home. I had picked up our daughter that morning, so I didn't get a chance to say much when she walked in. The ex-boyfriend brought a gun "just in case." Like I even cared at the moment.

The fights we have were now almost constant. We were just living together at this point. We called it quits about two months into the marriage. Which reminds me that I now have a pistol because my now ex-wife and I thought we should get our permit to carry. I pulled it out and cocked it. My hands started to get sweaty. All I could think about was that it had a hollow point, and I didn't want it to be a nasty scene. I couldn't tell you how many times I have held that gun with the thoughts of suicide on my mind. My drinking hit the fan. I was putting down a .750ml every day. I would drink from the moment I got the bottle till it was gone. I even had to start making sure I had enough so that I wouldn't run out. When I would have my daughter, I did everything in my power to make sure I wouldn't drink too much. I had to be alert enough to stay up still she was asleep and be able to wake up. Those nights turned into sleepless nights, and if I did get any sleep, I would have nightmare after nightmare.

I don't know how my body was taking all of this. I would show up to work on time. I was driving straight, not slurring my words, and nobody could tell the war going on behind the curtain. I had stopped talking to my friends at this point because they were the ones who wanted to get a shot at her or told me my wife was cheating. I wondered why they never said anything to her to have my back, so I didn't see any loyalty from them. Except one girl. She was dating my wifes' ex-boyfriend and had a thing with my best man from the wedding. Anyways, I started talking to her because we had something in common—we both really didn't like the new relationship that started between our now exes.

We started to date, and things went pretty well! We could sit and talk for hours. We would never run out of things to talk about. We loved going to concerts. We created a bond pretty fast. I think we helped each other through a bad breakup. I was still drinking, and the amount had stayed the same. Now I wasn't drinking to numb the pain; I was drinking to keep away the withdrawals.

A few weeks go by, and she had found my hiding spots. She wasn't mad at me, which really surprised me. She wanted to know why I was hiding it. She had been through enough situations in her life that she knew how to handle it. It was a breath of fresh air for me. Now I had someone I'm completely comfortable with and understands what I was going through and knows what caused all the pain. Now it was really time to quit. I would try and go days without alcohol, but I would always get so sick that I would have to skip work or spend the weekends that I didn't have my kid with me trying to make it five days without alcohol. My girl was always there to help with my daughter when I was trying to quit or not.

I ended up in the hospital again. This time I knew I was going to have to go. I wanted help this time. I did stay, and I was pumped full of vitamins and had no alcohol in my system. I got out, and I stayed sober for a month. I felt like I had control again. So I said, "Why not? You made it a month. It shouldn't be that bad to say no the next day." Well, that was the case till it turned to drinking every day again over a short couple of weeks.

I had screwed things up with my girlfriend by continuing to hide the alcohol and talking to my ex-wife again. I was so strung out and depressed about how I couldn't control myself. I couldn't even control my thoughts. I got the bright idea to try to take my life once again. This time I was drunk. Trying to tie a noose was difficult especially if you don't know how to. I got the rope and walked down to the shed that was on the property. My ex-girlfriend was in the house. I threw the rope up over the rafters and got it tight. I stood on top of my lawn mower and put the rope over my head. I leaned forward a little before leaning back. I took a breath and went forward. When I did, the knot didn't slide, and I basically was being held up by my chin, and the rope wasn't choking me to the point where I couldn't breathe. Now I have a dilemma. I can barely keep my toes on the lawn mower, and I was stuck. I had to call my ex-girlfriend to come down and push me back enough to get the rope that was squeezing the hell out of my head.

I told my now ex-girlfriend that we were better off friends. We kind of ended the dating aspect, and she moved out. So now I was alone at my house and trying to keep steady on the low amount that I have to drink a day. I was still lying to my family about being sober, but we have a trip to Mexico coming up the first week in March. I got my drinking down, and I was sober for about a week before we left so I wouldn't have to run into a problem getting there.

The trip to Mexico was awesome! It was an all-inclusive resort with a beach and tons of pools. They had a bunch of restaurants and stores, live entertainment, and nightlife spots. We got a catamaran and snorkeled and got to see the Mayan ruins. We even got to swim in ancient underground cave systems. The tree roots grew all the way through and had crystals everywhere. The food was decent, but the views were amazing. I was always up early and watched the sunrise. Also, I would be ready for the bar to open so I could get my double vodka orange juice. I hid the drinking from my family the whole trip. I wasn't getting drunk, and everyone else was saying they dilute the alcohol to stick to beer. I don't drink beer. It makes my stomach blow up, but what do I do anyway? I start drinking the beer from the fridge in the rooms because it had more alcohol in it. Overall, it was a great trip, and I learned a lot of the history of the land. Learned about the gods they worshiped and the human sacrifice rituals. I would recommend going because those caves were magical!

When I got back, I had another exciting thing coming up. I had plans to go to a EDM concert. The DJ was Subtonics, and definitely, he was one of my favorites. After the Mexico trip, I picked back up on the bottle, building up a tolerance over two weeks. The day of the concert was March 12. It was me, my ex-girlfriend, her nephew, and one of her good friends that were going. We got a hotel room in the cities so we didn't have to drive back after the concert. I picked them all up and had a half bottle of vodka. I thought I could make that last till the concert and have a little for morning to make it home. I finished most of it before we got to the concert, and I knew I was in trouble for the ride home, but we were getting molly, so I thought maybe I wouldn't be so bad. I was still hiding the alcohol because I didn't want my ex to think I was drinking again. I guess you could say I felt ashamed.

In the early hours of the morning, around 4:00 a.m., after an insane EDM concert, I started going through withdrawals. I've been through enough of them that I can almost get the exact time they will start and how much alcohol I need to feel sober again. To be honest, I have a personal breathalyzer and sadly .16 percent was sober to me. That day I was two hours from home and not a drop of liquor around me. Lucky for me, I was with a girl that knew of my addictions and who has been there for me through multiple withdrawals. I swear she is an angel. She rubbed my back between vomiting sessions and wiped the sweat from my back and neck. The other girl in the room was out cold. She had been drinking all night, and we had to pretty much carry her back to the hotel. So there was no waking her up. The guy that came with us was in a different room. Seven hours in my personal hell later, we finally hit the road. The problem is that we have a two hour drive till we get to town. It was obvious that I was in terrible shape, so I took the opportunity to start my recovery by admitting my addiction to the others and tell them I cant drive. I didn't make it far before they had to pull over for me.

We get back to town, and we still had to drop off everyone before I get dropped off at the emergency room for some reason, but I wasn't complaining. I could barely make up words and was lying in the back anyway. By the time I get into the hospital, I was shaking like I was having a seizure. The doctor and nurses already knew me, and my condition was the worst they had seen. On a side note, this was trip number four to the hospital for alcohol.. They got an IV in my arm, and I was finally feeling some relief. I beg the doctor to give me any medication to keep me away from the bottle, and he asked me if I was "for real this time." I immediately said yes because I honestly couldn't take another trip to the hospital.

After three days, I was released with about seven bottles of prescriptions and a newfound will to stay off alcohol and a new addiction to sugar. A few weeks went by, and I was showing some serious improvement. My family trusted that I was sober, and what friends I had left were proud of me. I felt like a new man. The medication was working and improving at work. I forgot one morning to take my medication for the cravings. I felt instant doom because I work twenty minutes from home, and there were plenty of liquor stores along the way. I didn't end up leaving work and spent the day thinking about the pill more than I did about alcohol, which seemed strange to me.

May 26 will always be a constant reminder of the rest of the story I have to share. The day started like most—get out of bed, take my meds, get ready for work, and head out. At the time, the medication I was taking was one for depression, one for anxiety, one for the cravings, and one for my shakiness. Something inside of me was saying that maybe I should see if I could go without my medication. I was not broken anymore. I've always hated relying on medication because I have been on antidepressants or anxiety meds since I was in high school. But I would quit all the time because I believe they were just sugar pills. Who knew? They could have been. Anyways, I said, "That's it," and went to work without them. The day went by, and all I could think was the craving pill and that I was craving something that was supposed to suppress the itch. It bothered me so much that when I got home, I took the pills and threw them all away.

On May 27, around 3:00 a.m. I got this stabbing pain in my stomach and started to get a little shaky. I was thinking, *Oh, it will go away in a bit, just drink some water.* After taking a drink of water, it was instant vomiting and dry heaving. I started to panic because this was happing all too fast. As I was trying to catch a breath between gags, I noticed myself going through withdrawal symptoms, but how could this be? I've been sober and eating like normal people do. My liver or something must be failing because this pain was unlike anything I ever felt. I made it to the toilet and felt my body start to shrink into a ball of tight muscles. My fingers didn't work, and if I move out of the fetal position, I felt like things would get worse. I used my elbow to get my phone out of my pocket. I have one of those passwords that has a pattern. Using my tongue, I unlocked and was able to dial my mom who lives just five miles away. It was 5:30 a.m. and I was praying to a God because that I didn't think she would answer.

My mom got the call and immediately stepped into action. She helped me down the stairs and into the vehicle. We now have a twenty-five-minute drive to the hospital. Life as I knew it was starting to fade in my eyes. I begged her to speed up and told her I can't do it anymore, that I need something to help this. She tried to comfort me by calling the emergency room to say we would need a wheelchair and that I needed immediate help.

We got to the hospital, and there wasn't anyone outside to cart me in, so my mother had to run in and grab one. I folded and, like a sack of potatoes, fell into the chair. I was rushed in, and the lobby was empty, just a secretary sitting on the other side of the glass. I got wheeled over to the desk, and she "*has to*" go through the symptoms for Covid 19. I told her, "Are you fucking kidding me? I have them all, now what?" She asked for my insurance and had me sign while I can't move my fingers. She put a wristband on my wrist and told me to wait.

A nurse came out and was shocked to see me in such a condition. I was wheeled right way to a room. By now all the nurses and doctors in the ER knew who I was because of all the trips I made the past couple of years. Well, that being said, they can't give me any medication till I get blood work done and a urine sample to check for drugs and alcohol. They got an IV in and took some blood, then left me there. My mom was in the room with me, and I could tell this was all hurting her. I pleaded that I have been sober and that I was not sure how much longer I was going to make it. I don't know what dying felt like, but I honestly thought this was it.

After what seemed like hours, the nurse came back in to check on me. She had nothing to give me and no time frame as to when I would get anything to help with the nausea and pain. I asked her to turn off the lights. The TV was on, so you could see the dimly lit room. I remember that was when I started to lose consciousness. My throat is completely raw from the violent vomiting. My uvula is so swollen that when I can manage a deep breath I can feel it moving on the back of my tongue causing me to gag. My stomach feels like its ripped open and I feel a warmth spreading through my body. I was begging for mercy for a while till I finally gave up and surrendered. My vision went to black and I got a feeling like no other. When I would slip out of consciousness I felt at peace and a state of complete surrender. Then all the sudden my body would jump up, and I would gasp like I was being brought back to life. I couldn't tell if I was wake or not because sometimes I would be dream that I woke up, but then I would jolt up again and actually be awake. This went on for some time. It felt like a sick, twisted joke. That was when I started talking to myself in my head, or out loud—I wasn't sure. Anyway, I used to talk to God like he was one of my voices in my head. I would have full on conversations with God, and I thought, *Hell, why not give it a shot? Because I felt like I was going to meet him anyways.* I closed my eyes and tried to put myself visually in a courtroom so I could plead guilty and say how sorry I was for whatever I did to deserve this. I felt nothing.

The doctor came in, looked at me, and read the charts. I had no clue how long anything was taking because being in the moment was the only place I could keep my mind. I was given medication for the pain and nausea, which felt like a breath of fresh air. It only made the pain tolerable. They then need a chest X-ray and a MRI, so I was carted off.

While I was being wheeled around, I kept drifting off, but they were trying to keep me awake. I had lost all sense of time, and being drugged up, I couldn't stand and could barely talk. Everyone was being so nice to me. I felt so vulnerable and weak. They were sticking needles in whenever they want and taking my blood. I didn't know what was happening anymore, so I was like a zombie being thrown through a giant tube at this point. I got but back on the bed and carted back to the emergency room.

It was around seven or eight at night when they told me that I was going to have to stay at the hospital till they can figure out what's going on. I got a room, and it was getting late. The doctor came in and started asking me questions. I probably got a couple words in before drifting off. I awoke again, and they had me sign a paper that I could leave. I could finally sleep.

Throughout the night I was getting stabbed as they drew blood every couple of hours. I remember waking up one time and my arm was sticking straight into the air and nobody was around. I don't know how long they let me sleep, for but when I woke up, I had shit the bed, and of course, there was a pretty nurse that had to take care of me for the day. I asked for something to change into, and all they had for me was a pair of women's underwear. I didn't come to the hospital with a change of clothes. I have not stood up in twenty-four hours, and believe me, you do not want to hear more about my getting out of bed. I got in the shower and had one of those typical shower scenes where you have your hands on the wall and your head under the water, except I had one arm sticking out of the shower to keep my IV dry. Anyways, that's when I realized that all I have is me to get me out of this hole that I have dug for myself. God blessed me with a shot at correcting my mistakes and reclaimed my imaginary friend that has helped push me through my childhood years. I felt really good, and I was starving! The nurse got me some stuff to drink, and I told her that felt brand new! I had to wait for the doctor to look at me before I could leave. He was baffled. He couldn't find anything that would have made me feel so much pain. He said that my body behaved like I had a bacterial infection but they didnt find anything. I got a ride home and I went to hang out at the lake with my family and family friends. They all asked me how I was feeling and what happened. I simply replied, "I have no idea."

It was early June now, and I felt some significant changes in my body. I did not crave sugar like I used to, and fast food made my stomach feel weird. I was working out every other day. I would get up early in morning and make coffee. I never really liked coffee, but now I was drinking it black. While I am drinking my morning coffee, I saw a TikTok about heyoka. I decided to look up the meaning, and I noticed a ton of similarities. A heyoka is a medicine man, someone that was working with the spirit world to bring safety to the tribe through visions or sudden thoughts that come from spirits or God himself.

After that, my "TikTok for You" page changed to clips about starseeds and light workers. I had no clue what they were, and with my newfound thirst for knowledge, I wasn't going to stop till I found out how I related to that. I was then thrown headfirst down a rabbit hole. I felt like I found something that nobody knows about!

I learned a lot while down in that rabbit hole, mostly about sacred traditional medicine and the spirit world. I learned about crystals and the healing powers that they have and also chakras and how they are aligned in the body. So now I constantly had my eyes on the lookout for cool rocks. Good thing I did because as I was working on myself, these rocks would show up in perfect synchronicity with what chakra I was working on. It was getting me so excited! I want to start telling people about my discovery. But when I would bring it up, nobody seemed to be as excited as I was.

I was spending a lot more time outside and working on the house. I have an old chicken coop that was half covered in vines, chipped paint, and a door that didn't work. It definitely needed some TLC. I decided to take the day off to fix it up and paint it.

While I was working on the coop, I started a new playlist on my Spotify, a bunch of old music I listened to in high school. It got me reminiscing of the things I wish I would have done after high school instead of what I did do. I had big dreams of being in a rock band and being a photographer. I had endless dreams. Living life to the fullest sounded like pure happiness. I also thought that it was impossible for me to achieve those dreams being that I was a nobody from a small town. Also, I was insecure.

As I was pulling weeds out, I noticed some cool rocks lined up along one of the sides; and of course, since I was fascinated with them and I had a new rock identifier app, I had to figure out what they were. But they weren't anything special. I then started on the weeds growing under the ramp to the door when I noticed one rock that was sitting perfectly on an old piece of wood. It was like someone had set it there. I picked it up, and it was pretty. It looked polished and had a dark-green color and speckled with other colors of green. The bottom side of it wasn't polished and was blackish in color. I didn't think to look it up because I was so busy, so I left it on a shelf inside the house. I finished the coop that day, and it looks amazing. I was proud of myself.

One day I got the urge to dig up some of the rocks that my lawnmower kept hitting. Not only where there a couple bowling-ball-sized rocks, but they were all so close together that I couldn't get the shovel to go very far in the dirt. After about ten rocks, I hit one in the center of the hole, which was about two and a half feet down. I started on that one as well because some of these rocks actually looked pretty cool. This one was different though. I just had to get it out. This rock was about the size of a one-year-old. I finally get the rock out and took it over to hose it off. When I did, they started to sparkle with billions of tiny gold flakes. Well, what else does a guy do other then try to break it open?

I hit that thing with an ax about a hundred times before it cracked. The inside of the rock is full of color and quarts lines. Ranging from black and gold flakes to the red and orange lines mixed with black. This thing is absolutely gorgeous. I remember that rock I found by the shed and decided to check it along with this new rock I found on the app. It told me it's a black tektite and that it's not a rock, it's space glass! Basically, a meteor fell from the sky and turned to glass going through the atmosphere. Well, that wasn't enough for me because it looked like it was set where I found it. After an extensive search, I come to find out that in Native American culture, a heyoka would leave one when they passed. The big rock turned out to be a sediment rock, and I couldn't get a good reading, but this thing had to be special, so I made it into an altar that I set up on my porch. Now I can meditate and watch the sunrise and feel like a real heyoka.

When I started to meditate, I felt like I was doing it wrong, when really there isn't a wrong way. The simple act of sitting down and trying to quiet your mind is meditation. We do it all the time! I have found that paying attention to the breathing is a good start. Count the breaths in—one, two, three, four. Then count the breaths out—one, two, three, four. Also notice the pause between breaths. Whenever a negative thought is presented, try to bring the focus back on the counting. Like anything else, practice makes better. Being able to quiet the mind gives us an opportunity to face our negative thoughts and see them from a different perspectives. One way to a happy life is the ability to handle emotions.

A week later I was trying to contact anybody in the Native community for help on the subject. Being half Norwegian/Swedish on my mother's side and not sure about my father's (I think he is French), I felt completely uncomfortable, and it didn't help when I tried to talk to my parents about it. They would say, "Well, you aren't Native." They weren't sure what I was doing, and they didn't want me to be disrespectful. I didn't either, but curiosity overcame the fear. I had to know more. I called as many reservations as I could and emailed them. I didn't get any answers. Eventually, I got ahold of one gentleman, and he told me not to be so worked up and that he knew of another medicine man. He got me calmed down a bit, but I wasn't given much since in that culture, it's all about self-discovery.

Now I had an urge to figure out what was going on with me and with all the energy and mind power that I have. Then I learned of a man named Black Elk. He is a medicine man and has published a book. I read that book front to back in just a couple of days! I felt like I was going crazy now because there were way too many similarities between me and him. We are both half blind; had visons or gut feelings that the world isn't really on the same page as mother earth; and was shot in the rib cage, leaving a nasty cut. I have a three-inch bad cut on my ribs as well.

I went to work the next day. It was going as usual, but business slowed down at the shop, so I was the only one left for the day. I was watching documentaries on ancient periods of time when I started to feel my eyes getting heavy. I started to feel like I was dreaming, but my eyes were open. I got in this daydream state. Then a story just started flowing through me, so I started trying to write everything down I saw and drew quick pictures as the dream carried on. At the end of it, I look down at everything and realized I had my first vision, just like Black Elk.

The vision started with me curled up in a ball on the frozen ground with no clothes on but some boxers. Deep in the woods, I was next to a ring of rocks that made a fire pit. There were some logs in the ring, but no fire, and the logs were collecting snow. I had a few matches, but I knew they were no good. I felt misery and despair. I noticed I was shaking and had an upset stomach. The snow was falling. Knowing that I was not going to make it, I put my head down in the snow and started to cry and accepted that I was going to die. A moment went by when I felt a presence. I lifted my head a little and noticed that the snow around me was melting. I was not cold anymore, so I stood up and looked around. The night sky was shimmering with millions of stars peeking from the trees above me. Two clouds came rolling in, but they were only twenty feet above me like ghostly fog. They started to rain, but the raindrops were rainbow colored, soaking the fire in front of me. I got this overwhelmingly blissful tingle moving up my spine, and I heard a voice telling me to turn around. When I did, I saw a lit candle. The flame was blue with a green aura. The voice said, "Take this," and as I did, the voice said, "Throw it on the fire, but be prepared because it's going to be bright!" I tossed it, and it was so bright that all I saw was pure white light.

As the light faded, I noticed I was on a stage speaking. I looked down, and I was barefoot. When I looked up, it looked like the original Wood stock of '69. Everyone was happy. It was one huge community of like-minded people. Then I snapped out of it.

I had to go tell my parent about this dream. I tried to interpret it the best I could. At the end of it, I told them I want to be a motivational speaker, which is something I have wanted to do for a while, but I just always get stage fright and would jumble up all my words. They noticed my excitement and were happy to see me so happy.

The next day I went online to try find someone that will tell me what was going on with me. I found a website with life coaches. I arranged a meeting with a life coach to get me on a direct path or at least, an end goal. She noticed how excited I was, and I started to think, *Hey, I could be a life coach.* The lady told me to keep a journal and write down my thoughts and dreams so I could go back and not have to try to remember everything. Well, I never journaled before but thought, *Hey, why not?*

This lady might me on to something. I searched my place for a notebook to start and found an old sketchbook that I kept since high school. The looked at the first page and laughed because I had been practicing my professional signature and had a couple of the nineties' cool *S* symbols kids would draw, but hey, it was perfect.

A few days went by, and I got an email from a lady named Bunny Sings Wolf. She was a heyoka! I found her page, and she had run into the same problem as me. She's a small-framed women with red hair and light skin. I was full of questions, and she was nice enough to have a chat with me. She told me about Crazy Horse and his vison. She talked about her vison, and when I brought up Black Elk, she seemed joyful I said it. I knew of Crazy Horse from the book about Black Elk, which got us thinking we met for a reason. After that, I got the urge to go climb the mountain that Black Elk had in his vision for the future of his people. So I planned a spontaneous trip to the Black Hills on that Friday.

Friday came, and I came to work, but I was hoping I could get the day off so I could go for my trip. Surprisingly, I got the day off. My dad even gave me a few extra bucks! I got in my truck and headed home to pack and grab my dog, Gus. Before I left, I wanted to make a video of the start of my new adventure with the thoughts of being a motivational speaker at some point. I made the video, then headed out. You can find the video on YouTube! (https://youtu.be/5GOeuSEldN0).

I typed in "Black Elk peak," and I learned that it was a nine-and-a-half-hour trip. What better opportunity than to do some research on others like me. I came across a man talking about transpersonal phenomena, and I thought that sounded a lot like me. Basically, the theory is that when a person goes through life and has a large amount of trauma without dealing with the emotions, a sudden moment expands your consciousness, and it takes only a moment in traffic or a gaze into a sunrise and your little bubble that you called life is shattered. Everything you used to believe is all the sudden flipped. You have to forget everything you knew and relearn everything about yourself. You are forced into this higher conscience and given truths about the world that everyone else is blind to. The researcher explained how you're given information about the world through spirits, frequencies and the rays of the sun.

Well, that sounded like me, so I pulled out the camera again to make a short video on my discovery. I also told the imaginary crowd how I hope that I get downloads of information from the sun and that I hope that when I get to the top of the mountain that would I get a huge download so I can tell the world of this discovery.

I finally get to the mountain, and for the last hour, I didn't know if I stayed on my side of the road for more than two minutes because the view was so beautiful. I was constantly stopping and taking pictures. I thought that I haven't been this happy in many years. Anyways, I got to the park and jumped out of the truck. The air smelled so fresh, and there was a small lake in front of me. I would have never imagined a lake on a mountain, but it was stunning. I got my stuff together, and we set out on the trail. One thing I noticed right away was all the crystals on the ground. I could feel this energy giving me the motivation to keep going till I got to the top. When I was almost to the peak, I met two guys, and they had told me I only had a few minutes because it was getting to the end of the day and there is a two-hour hike back down the mountain.

I got to the top of the peak, and a storm came through. Lightning and thunder on a mountain peak are ten times more intense! In the book, I read that Black Elk would speak to the thunder gods, so I felt that they were there with me congratulating me on my journey so far. I stayed for a little bit and took in the views. After that, I started running down the mountain with Gus. I was soaking wet because the rain was coming down like bullets, and the path was filling with water. I caught up with the guys that I met on the way up somehow. We walked together back down and shared stories and come to find out that they too were on a spontaneous trip and never hiked a mountain just like me!

On the drive there and back, I decided to make some motivational videos so I can share with the world my discovery so far. Before making the video, on the way back, I had a moment where I felt like my inner child was coming back to life. All I could think of was how I had kept myself from doing all the things I wanted to do when I was younger because I didn't believe I could. Nobody told me, "Hey, you will never be able to do that." It was only me, so I cried happy tears because now I know why I haven't done anything with my life. It was me all along telling myself I'll never make it. Now I'm determined to make the best of my life.

When I got back, it was like 7:00 a.m., so I took a nap. I had a very lucid dream. I was walking along the road and noticed a lady was running up to me, ranting that she has made this discovery of the world. I told her I had the same experience, but a little wiser now, I got her to calm down and talked her through what I knew. The dream felt so real because I was actually talking and not just watching things happen.

It all felt surreal, but it was making sense to Bunny Sings Wolf, so I know I'm on to something. I had a Zoom call with her, and I told her all about it. While I was waiting, I decided to draw a picture in my journal. It was a sketch of the tree of life and something I usually doodle when I'm bored. She tells me she is creating an app so she can teach the sacred medicine traditions and heal the world the traditional ways. I showed her the drawing, and she wanted a picture of it! I gladly gave it to her. She wanted to use it for her app. I felt honored.

A couple days later I remembered that my house has a plaque out front. On this plaque states the date of the first parochial school built by Neil Peterson, a man who fought in the Dakota War in 1862. Now this was an interesting discovery. I had to look up the history of the land I live on, and I found out that there was a battle that happened on West Norway Lake in Minnesota. The battle happened at the very beginning of the Dakota War. I told my parents about the awesome find, but they didn't see the significance of it the way I did since learning about heyoka. So I let it go.

The app Bunny Sings Wolf wasn't up yet, and I can't stop this new addiction for knowledge, so I search the web for natural medicine and energy healing. I stumbled across The Awake Academy. I signed up right away. I got a loan, only because Dr. Rebecca Sullivan had made sure I would get it. It changed my life! With that class, I was healed of all my childhood and adult trauma. She had a meditation at the end of each session using frequencies, binaural beats, and healing energy. I was completely blown away at the results. It absolutely worked. I also learned of the chakra system used by yogis.

There are seven main chakras. It all starts with the first chakra, which is the root chakra. The root/Earth chakra is responsible for basic survival needs: (in hierarchy) thirst, hunger, tiredness, security, money, and pain. So if that chakra is out of whack, then you have problems. Symptoms of blockage include leg or feet problems, eating disorders, constipation, lack of energy, feeling lethargy, and feeling ungrounded.

The second chakra is the sacral chakra. This chakra is related to your ability to feel pleasure, joy, connectiveness with others, creativity and ability to accept change. Once you have this one open, your world is flipped for the better. Symptoms of blockage include constipation, urinary problems, infertility, depression, fear, jealousy, and addictive behavior.

The third chakra is the solar plexus. This chakra is responsible for your physical and emotional power, your sense of identity, will power, and the command of respect from others. Basically, you become confident! Symptoms of blockage can include digestion issues, feeling powerless, aggressive behavior, victim mentality, and lack of confidence.

The fourth chakra is my favorite. It's the heart chakra! This chakra is responsible for your sense of inner peace, unconditional love, and service to others. Basically, this helps you show compassion for others, which is so important in the world we live in right now. Symptoms of blockage include hypertension, cardiovascular problems, overextending yourself, no personal boundaries, overly critical, and lacking empathy.

The fifth chakra is the throat chakra. This chakra is responsible for your sense of expression, ability to communicate and speak your truths. What I mean by speaking your truth, I mean the ability to live and speak your truth without fear. Symptoms of blockage include lack of control over one's speech, poor listener, difficulty to express feelings, headaches, dental issues, and lack of purpose in life.

The sixth chakra is the third-eye chakra. This chakra is related to your ability to understand truth, your wisdom, creativity, and inspiration. Symptoms of blockage include migraines, seizures, poor vision, poor memory, hallucinations, and insomnia.

The seventh chakra is the crown chakra. This chakra is responsible for your connection to spirituality, clarity of thoughts, and peace. They say this is the chakra related to enlightenment. It is the sense of universal knowledge, wisdom, and connection to the higher power. It is otherwise known as the meditation chakra. Symptoms of blockage include loneliness, lack of direction, neurological disorders, Alzheimer's, schizophrenia, depression, and insomnia.

When all of these are aligned and working in perfect harmony, it creates what they call a Christ conscience. The ability to live life the way Jesus and other ascended masters. Ascended masters are high-vibrational beings of love and light. Others include the Mother Mary, Buddha, St. Francis, etc.

During my classes, I downloaded an app called Gaia. Oh boy, was that useful. It really opened my ways of thinking; and I spent more time learning about stars, space, truths, lucid dreams, and ancient civilization than I did sleeping. Since the hospital, I haven't had to sleep more than four hours because meditation and a new diet supplied all I needed and more.

At work, my dad noticed how much I have changed and was proud of me. So he said he was giving me a raise! In the back of my mind, I wanted to quit. This new life I found has nothing to do with work and my old life. So coming into work is hard because all I wanted to do was find out more and more about myself and the rest of the world. I've been working for my dad on and off since I graduated. It was always been a safety net for me.

While researching on Gaia, I got on the topic of the Bible. The things they were saying about it made complete sense to me. Having my chakras lined up in harmony, I was able to understand the truth that the Bible is more than just information on how the world came to be. It includes teachings on how to live a compassionate life, just like Jesus did, so you can make it to heaven. I also learned that there were books left out by the Roman Catholic Church to create chaos, like the book of Enoch. I was so blown away because when I was younger, I made God my best friend. He was like an imaginary friend that would go on adventures with me, and I would tell stories to him. I would cry to him and tell jokes and laugh at myself. Well, growing up in a Christian family, the Bible is looked at differently, and I had the understanding that God was something else, not like that buddy I had made him up to be. So I guess that's where I lost my way. The only time I would run to God after that was when I was either going to kill myself or thank him for not letting me die after a drinking binge full of drugs. God used to be a man in the sky and now God exists all around me and in everyone around me.

Now I have a serious problem. My heart is telling me I have been right my entire life and I have lived this terrible life since I abandoned my faith. My entire family believes every single word in the Bible as its written. My uncle is even a pastor. I don't know what to think. On one side of my life, I see nothing but happiness and a positive outlook on life. The other side is my life of twenty-nine years, which had been a lie. I love every single one of my family members, but telling them I don't believe what they believe and quitting the family business when I basically have to run the daily work at the shop makes me sick to my stomach. With the roller coaster of emotions, I feel stuck. So I asked God to be my best friend again. Boy, am I glad I did! I am starting to see angel numbers like I did in high school. This time they make sense! I sat down and told God, "God I am at the fork in the road of my life. I need you to help guide me down the righteous path." He answered, and I have never felt so loved in my life. Angel numbers started popping up. I'm now writing down all my angel numbers I see and the advice that they give to me has brought me to a new discovery about myself.

For those who have never heard of angel numbers, an angel number is a sequence of numbers, for example, 1111, 2222, or random ones like one of the ones that followed me all my life is 1143. They are the ways that angels can give to hint us at the direction that our life is going is the right path uniquely for us. By typing them into Google, you can find various answers, and you determine if it resonates with you and your life journey.

The night I made my conclusion about the Bible, I had another lucid dream. It started with me wandering the streets at night in a kind of run-down neighborhood. I stumbled across a house party. I walked inside and didn't know anyone really, but a group of people grabbed me and ushered my into a room of like seven people. This dude that looked like the Asian guy from the movie *Disturbia* gave me some magic mushrooms. After I took them, the conversation turned to getting in a van. So we hopped in and started driving. As we were driving, I was looking out the window, and I was watching the scenery changing to waves of rainbow colors. I looked over my side to express the awe that

I was in, and the person I was talking to was a lady. She got a kind of curly brown hair and glasses, but her expression on her face was priceless. She was smiling cheek to cheek. I told her that I was seeing the colors! What she said back to me I would never forget. She said, "It's the hairless eyelids!" I laughed and turned back to look at the mountains and trees. Then I blacked out, and I was back in the room where I took the shrooms. I was hunched over on the floor next to the Asian dude's bed. I looked up, and he had this look on his face like I was crazy. I got the feeling that the night didn't go so well. I asked him what happened, and he told me I got a little out of control, but that happens to all of us.

He brought me my stuff and ushered me downstairs. I was stopped by some security, and there was a big metal door that they opened. I was shoved out. The sky was gray, and it was like an apocalypse had just happened. As soon as I got out, I felt like I was in danger, so I ran to the first car I saw, but I couldn't get in. All the sudden, I was getting kidnapped and shoved in another van. We made it to our destination. They opened the door, and I stepped out. I saw a big lake surrounded by gravel. The sky was cloudy and gray. They pushed me forward and told me I'd be able to see this dragon. Then all of a sudden, this tornado comes flying in, but it turned out to be a dragon with swirling dust and water. It noticed me, and when it did, it seemed it got scared and flew away. They put me back into the van and brough me back to the sketchy house. I walked in, and everything was cleaned up. I was introduced to a team, then they told me I messed up this girl's room and the *Disturbia* guy let me use his. I felt welcomed. I then woke up.

Out of curiosity, I wanted to know if my dreams had any clues as to why I was going through this awakening. What I found was, Satan was described to be a dragon and that Thor, the god of lightning and thunder, defeated the world serpent in mythology.

It was September 5, 2022, and I was sitting on my meditation mat outside, looking at the stars by the altar that I had made out of that big rock I had dug up. I had just finished doing a spirit guide meditation when I opened my eyes and saw that two of my candles were out. I have four candles representing air, fire, earth, and water. The only ones lit were the air and earth. I felt like it represented my connection with mother earth and God in the sky.

I thought it might be a good time to get another module done for class, and the subject we are on was about cleansing houses and objects from evil spirits. Knowing that there was a bloody day on the land that I live, I felt it was a good one to learn. As I was watching the video, all of a the sudden a black box covered most of my vision. I blinked a few times, and it was still there. Now I was rubbing my eyes, but it was not going away. About twenty seconds went by, and then it was gone.

I started to think maybe it was a symbol from my spirit guide. I then went into a deep meditation. During my meditation, I met my spirit guide. It was a light being dressed in shimmering white robes with a hood that covered the face, enough that there was a shadow over the eyes. Then this being looked at me. I could see crystal-blue eyes that looked that they were smoldering a bit. He had big angel wings! I vocalized that I needed help with all of this because now it was getting scary. I then felt a wave of calm rush over me. I opened my eyes, and the box was back, except this time an omega symbol was there. I blinked a few times, and all it did was make it flash. Five seconds later, it was all gone.

After that, I was determined to figure out what that all meant. I gathered all my things and went inside. I was totally in shock at the moment, and I looked down at my dog, Gus. I asked him, "Did you see that?" Laughing nervously, I sat down at the table and did my search.

The omega symbol in Christianity comes from the book of Revelations where Jesus said, "I am the alpha and the omega, the beginning and the end." In astrology, the alpha and omega symbol is used to explain the lunar nodes. A lunar node is either of the two orbital nodes of the moon. The two points at which the orbit of the moon intersects in the ecliptic hemisphere. Omega is related to Pisces. Pisces is the twelfth astrology sign. Omega is the twenty-fourth letter of the Greek alphabet, meaning they are the last position and time of destruction, change, and rebirth. So why did I get that symbol from my spirit guide? I learned that the moon was in Pisces last September 10, 2022. So basically, my guide was telling me to put an end to something.

You would think that someone who is going through all this mental stress and being alone for five months with no one but your dog and a daughter half of the week would drive one to go crazy, but I've never been more comfortable. I almost never want to leave the house because of all the good things that were happening to me when I follow my heart. And I was starting to love myself more and more. All of this is so fascinating to me, but my problem is, nobody understands when I talk about it.

September 8 rolled around, and I noticed an angel number. I went to look it up, and it said I was now given the gift to hear angels. That ringing in your ear can either mean you have bad ears or it can be angels. The spiritual meaning behind the ringing is often a sign that you have clairaudient or clairsentient abilities. This means you are able to discern energies around you. You are considered HSP, or a highly sensitive person, an empath of sorts. A high-pitch ringing in the right ear means a spiritual being is coming in on your crown chakra. These are usually beings of light or angels. A low-pitch ringing in your right ear means there is a presence of a spirit of negative energy is coming in on your lower chakras. A buzzing or white noise in your right ear could mean a strong attachment to someone or something like a pet or object. A sudden loud ringing means, "Pay attention, this could be good or bad." High-pitch ringing in your left ear is a sign that you are in a growing period, stepping into a higher vibration. Your energy is recalibrating. A low-pitch ringing in the left ear is a sign that a negative energy is causing an off balance in your chakras. Buzzing or white noise in the left ear is a message from your higher self, especially if you are accompanied by a feeling of trust or peace, meaning that the communication pathways between you and your higher self are opening. Your intuitive language is developing. A sudden loud ringing will mean the same. You can quiet the ringing by saying out loud "I hear you" to the energy coming in.

It was September 9, the night before the full moon, and I got the idea to try and lift the veil to the spirit world by taking some acid. Scientists, therapists, and holistic healers use these psychedelics in trauma treatments because it expands your way of thinking, giving you the ability to see yourself from a different perspective. Usually, you are not as judgmental of yourself, and it helps cope with different mental illnesses. When I did, I had a blast. I lay outside and put on my headphones. I listened to hours of Alan Watts. I recommend you listen to one of his talks. It really changes your way of thinking.

The next day I took a trip to see a guru. I have been watching a guru named Sadguru, and he is great. I thought I would give it a shot. The talk that he had was on the topic of true happiness. It was very inspirational. I was the only White guy covered in tattoos, so I stuck out like a sore thumb, but everyone made me feel very welcome. I am not sure why I was so nervous. Maybe it was because the country seems to be getting divided by race, and I thought I would make everyone else uncomfortable.

A couple days went by, and I was starting to feel a bit lonely since I haven't really had any friends since March. So I got on Facebook dating. I was eventually match with a girl. Of all names, Crystal! She was saying she needed help moving to a new place, so I offered the help. We met, and I could tell right away she had a dark past. We got to talking, and she completely opened up. I was shocked, but I heard what she had to say. She told me that it usually pushes people away, but I didn't care, I could see the beautiful soul underneath. I asked her about her tattoos, and we got to talking about art and such. I kept in contact with her for a bit afterward, and I noticed that she was starting to change. She was singing in the car on Snap and looked like she was really starting to love life. That when I remembered when Dr. Sullivan had said that I would be able to start changing people for the better just by being around them with a positive vibe. It's now making sense. I am a healer!

On September 14, while scrolling on Facebook, I saw an ad for becoming a public speaker with zero experience. If that isn't a sign from

God, then I don't know what is. So I jumped on it. I got in on a live chat with the guy talking about his business, and he was looking for people that have a message for the world. I applied right away, and boom, they want to talk. I gave them a time after work. I got the call. They said there must have been a mix up with the schedule, and my mind said, *Stop, this is a sign God doesn't want me to share what I discovered*. So I said, "Hey, thank you, but I'm going to pass."

A couple days passed, and I got a call from a random number. I decided to answer. It was the guys from the speaking company! Now I realized that I let my self-doubting thoughts get in the way of a huge opportunity. God wasn't going to let me down. I *must* do this now. If I could get on a stage and voice the journey I've been on, I could change the world. With God, possibilities are endless. I could help people recover from addiction by introducing meditation practices or the many natural medicine practices that actually work, but most of all, I am giving God the steering wheel. The system put in place for mental health is going to change!

While getting ready with my speech, I had trouble finding out how my journey is going to help or how I can incorporate it into one topic. Another problem was that I can't explain what I had been through within a simple fifteen-minute speech. I decided to go back into my journal, which by now had fifty plus pages of dreams, prayers, messages from angels, ah-ha moments, and personal affirmations. I found out that it would be very difficult to incorporate all that in a fifteen-minute time frame, so I thought I should just write a book. Then when I thought more about it, I seemed like I kind of already have in my journal.

—⁓—

I've been told that we always have multiple angels or ascended masters around us, and I have been writing down all of the ones I come across that resonated with me and my life. I decided I wanted to find out if there were any saints that related to my mental health issues that could possibly be helping me along. That's when I discovered St. Dymphna. She is the patron of runaways, mental disorders, neurological disorders, incest victims, and sexual assault victims. So I wrote that down, and now I am reciting the prayer associated with her. I pray for all victims, and if you are one of them, I got your back. I'm praying for you.

While at work, I get the urge to go to Green Lake Bible Camp. I got there, took off my shoes, and sat under a tree. I meditated for a bit and started to write all the stories I wanted to share with the world. One of the stories that came up was the time I came here. It's a pretty special place to me. This was the place I went before going to my parents' cabin to commit suicide.

Anyway, when I got out and found that heart, I put it in a book and up on a shelf. I wanted to share that story for a while but couldn't find the book to prove my point. I forgot about that story till now. So I wrote it down. I looked up, and the tree I was sitting under has a branch that looked like a stick man pointing at the church. At this point I was seeing signs from God everywhere. I see angel numbers and communicate constantly, so I went to look what it was pointing at. It was a prayer walk. So I did the walk and sat in the middle. I sat in silence, praying to know why me and what was I supposed to be doing with all of the information I have. I waiting to get an answer. I waited and waited but didn't get anything. I wasn't discouraged when I didn't get anything because my dreams usually gave me answers I was looking for or sudden thoughts that turned out to be true.

That night I had a dream about a boat sitting in the sand and an angry-looking man in an all-yellow rain suit. I asked him if I was dreaming like I usually do to get myself to lucid dream. I looked down and felt a cuff or chains break away from my ankles, and I grew wings and the sky got rainy and dark. I flew for a bit, but I couldn't control it very well since I have never been able to fly in my lucid dreams. After that, I was in an apartment building hallway knocking on a door when a guy with a bag of white powder and all sorts of strung out answered. He jumped on me and tried to kiss me and lick my face. I pushed him off and got up. I wasn't mad at all because I know what it was like to not be myself. So I asked him if he wanted help. He looked at me and then walked away all normal. Then the dream jumped to me walking down the street with a bunch of kids in my old high school class. We were all excited for some reason. Then that was it. I woke up.

When I woke up, I jumped in the shower to get ready. When I was scrubbing, I noticed my two silver necklaces that I always have on were missing! I never take them off, with one of them I can't even hardly get over my head. The clip was also bent, so it won't come off that way either. I jumped out because it couldn't be possible. I looked on my bed, and there they were lying next to where I slept.

A couple of days later I wanted to go back to the prayer walk and try to see if God could explain a little better since I still didn't know what to say in my speech. Before my walk, I sat down on a boulder to write my thoughts before praying. As I was writing, all I could think about was that story with the heart and wishing I could find the book where I had placed that heart in. Well, on the next page was a baby marijuana leaf. That got me thinking. I did hear somewhere that Jesus liked marijuana! Not sure that's true, but that's not what was so profound. What I realized was that the book I have been using was a book I took from my house after I graduated. I have been writing in the same book I put the heart in so long ago and couldn't find it because it wasn't there anymore. My brain put together twelve years of things that didn't make sense to me in about five seconds.

I made a full circle. From wanting to die and asking God to stop me to begging God to tell me what I can do to uphold my duties as a man chosen to communicate with the spirit realm. I looked down, and there was a pine cone. I looked up for the symbolism, and it said that it symbolized enlightenment.

I still didn't have an answer with regards to the message I wanted to share the world, and I was getting frustrated trying to explain to my parents, who were also are my employers, why I wanted to focus all my energy on the new site I made and in writing a book. My vehicle and cell phone were from them, I rent my house from them, they paid for my speech class, and I still owe them $7,500 in debt for hospital bills. I can't get them to understand how important it is that I was communicating with spirits. My heart is split. I can't give up on this journey, and I can't afford to live without a job.

I did see a TikTok that was pretty interesting. It went something like, let's say you walk into a room where you get a sense of negative emotion. Well, that can be explained. If people understood the power of consciousness and a mass consciousness, they would be able to completely change the direction of the planet. I think that it's a big secret the intelligence community is hiding. There is a link between the collective consciousness and the physical world. Sociology studies were done where they would go into communities of let's say two hundred thousand people. They would then send in 1 percent of that population (so two thousand people). These two hundred people would go into a deep meditation.

What they found was that emergency room visits declined, violent crimes declined, robberies and all sorts of negative activity declined, even though they those people didn't know that the two thousand were in the city. There is this resonate effect that I like to call the force or an entangled and interwoven consciousness field. And people who didn't know these meditators were there became more ordered, more peaceful, happier, and so on.

This study was based on quantum physics in which a container of helium was cooled down to absolute zero. When 1 percent became aligned to go, the entire container went through this transition, instantly shifting into coherence and taking on almost magical properties. It is a state called superfluidity. So there is this transition at the 1 percent. So when a critical mass of people, whether its 1 percent or a fraction of that (depends on the ones practicing the meditation or prayer), you can shift an entire civilization. If we can become coherent like the 1 percent and we become aligned in coherence, moving the right direction, it will transform the other 99 percent even though they didn't even know we're doing it. That's the beauty and power of community and collective consciousness. How crazy is that?

I went home and rolled a cigarette, then I went outside to walk of some of the anxiety. I went to look at the hole where I got the altar rock, and I noticed a red feather sitting in the hole. A red feather symbolizes strength and vitality. It cheered me up a bit. I sat in the dirt and took some deep breaths. The breeze picked up. I got goose bumps. All the sudden a flock of crows landed on the tree above me, covering every branch, and they were so loud. I got another overwhelming thought. I visualized my house being a sanctuary for animals. I would add fencing, a horse barn, a kenneling area for dogs. It would be a place where people can drop off their pets and go on a vacation. My house and land would offer my healing services. I would also add solar panels and a greenhouse. Living off the land, writing books, and helping others sounds like heaven to me.

That got me thinking about the plaque on the front of my house. So I went back to take a look at it again since I haven't thought about it for a few months. I started to do some research. I found out the first pastor that held services there. His name was Pastor Andrew Jackson. He was a thirty-three-year-old Swedish man. In 1852, he made his way to Waupaca, Wisconsin, and joined some Swedes and became a schoolmaster for the fall and winter term of 1858–1859 until he moved to Minnesota the summer of 1859. He met Rev. Peter Carlson, who traveled with him to Kandiyohi County. Andrew found a spot on West Norway lake that he wanted to call home.

On July 1861 there was a meeting for the five parishes. There were three Swedish parishes: Eagle Lake, Nest lake, and West Norway Lake. The two of the Norwegian speaking ones consisted of Crow River and Norway Lake. The area reminded them of home, so they called the organization New Sweden.

On August 10, 1861, they held a service at the Norway Lake church. They assigned a six-person board of deacons: Swen Borgen, Johannes Lundborg, Ole Knudson, Evan Railson, Johannes Haavelson, and Tomas Osdmuson (if anything was happening, Tomas was there). A few days later, they would be pronounced the trustees.

On August 17, 1861, the first church service under the newly constituted and easily recognized congregational entity was held. Andrew Jackson enjoyed the Norwegian company, and they liked him, more so the Norwegian pastors. Jackson would make the rounds at the different parishes, and while on one of the trips, he ran into a party of Sioux Indians that had set up camp on Lake Henderson, which was a favorite hunting spot. Jackson then spoke briefly with the legendary chief Little Crow.

On August 20,1862, Andrew would have two services. Young Bergit Osdmuson, part of the Norwegian parish, was ready for worship services at her cabin along with her sister's congregation. These two had social status. Andrew was officiating the service. He was facing his congregation when terrible news had reached the cabin. The West Norway Lake were attacked, and many were dead. Unknown to everyone, the 1862 Dakota War had just broken out and was headed toward Kandyohi County.

I remembered that there is a little tiny church up on a hill about a mile away. I went there one time while in my drunken stupor and accidently bumped a tree with my truck as I was trying to go around it. I went because I wanted to pray for my sins, but anyway, I drove straight there! I now have all of this information, and I find the plaque that said, "Pastor Andrew Jackson." I couldn't believe it. I took some pictures of the land, and it was beautiful, especially with the leaves changing. I could see why they named it New Sweden.

It was now October 5. I had been feeling some anxiety all day, so I did what a know best—I went for a hike! There is nothing like the smell of fall with all the colors. So I set out. I had never been to the lookout tower, so I thought that would be a good destination. On this hike, I had absolutely no idea how to walk the trails, so I followed my intuition. I came across some turkeys and found a turkey feather. The spirit of the turkey is the connection with earth, connection with the spirit of the land, importance of community, and harvesting fruits of your efforts. I thought that was pretty neat being that I was trying so hard to share my ideas.

The next day I was feeling like I have to be on to something, but I wasn't feeling too confident in my ability to connect with the spirits, so I sat down and prayed. I showed my gratitude and meditated. I decided to roll a cigarette again and walked the property, trying to visualize setting up the Recovery Ranch. That's when a flock of crows came back, and there were so many more this time. They would follow me from each big oak tree to oak tree. I got chills, and I felt a presence, so I put my hands on the tree and took some deep breaths. My head started to feel a pulse. That's when all the crows got dead silent. It lasted only three or four seconds, but after that, they all got up and flew away. That was surreal.

Looking for ways to communicate better I looked up "heyoka lifestyles." I got to reading and heard about power animals. A power animal is one that chooses you. You can't say, "I want this as a power animal." That got me thinking of animals that have always been around me. Then I thought of a chipmunk. I had always had one around at the cabin and around my house that I called Tiny Tim, but no, it didn't really match my life story. So I got the idea of birds. I have always been scared of things that fly like birds and bats and butterflies and what not. That reminded me of the time a raven chased me down. I was hitting golf balls at the range and went out to go pick the balls up. I think the raven wanted the golf ball because I was running and screaming, and this bird wouldn't give up. So then I threw it! I also didn't like the show *That's So Raven*, which is funny because the raven in the show was a psychic. My favorite sports team for football is the Ravens. Now that I think of it, ravens have been part of my journey all the way up till now. I had a call from a lady named Raven at the shop, and the phone number she gave me had an angel number on it. When I looked up the number, it had to do with the Bible story of Noah and the ark (when Noah sent out a raven).

I decided to look up what a raven meant as a power animal. What I found was pretty life- changing. In Native American culture, the raven brings us to a higher awareness of our inner working, our conscious and unconscious. He is a silent observer of his environment. The raven is persistent and will find a way to untangle the knots woven in a lifetime so inner truths may be revealed.

I looked into it a little further, and the raven has some folklore to it. There is a really cool story behind it. The raven is known as the creator of light and as a trickster. I suggest looking the stories up. Anyways, now I understand what I was put on earth to do and what I had to learn.

I learned that life is all about choices. I have made more than my fair share of mistakes. You can't fix the past and moving forward is the only option. The choices you make, make your future. If you're not happy with what you have chosen, you have two options: learn from it and make better choices or keep beating yourself up about it and let it drag you through the dirt till you let go. I have learned the hard way what its like to people please to the extent to living separate lives and how holding emotions and feelings to yourself can actually build up and change your life. I learned that the voice in your head Isn't you. You are the observer of your thoughts. You have a choice in how you react so take a breath before you make a choice. I learned that the only thing constant in the world is change. Whether you like it or not, it happens. It's something you have to flow with. Trying to resist just causes problems so make the best of it. I learned that sometimes you have to swallow your pride and ask for help. You need to love yourself enough to get the help you need. Trying to quit an addiction on your own can kill you. I learned that my chronic digestive problems, depression, anxitiy, nightmares and suicidal thoughts since I was sixteen were cured by taking a few months to balance my Mind, Body, and Spirit. I learned that ego is the defense built up to keep you safe and shields you from showing true emotion. Ego is the only thing keeping you from being who you truly are. Being who you truly are gives your life purpose, and living your purpose creates bliss. Most of all, I learned that our creator is gracious. No matter what you have done, he accepts you for who you are so be yourself.

What I am here to do is to heal myself and help others heal. By exposing my truth, I hope to inspire others to live a meaningful life. I hope this raises awareness for the mental health crisis we are in and the sacred healing approach that truly lasts. Some sacred practices are proven to improve overall health beyond recovery. Some you can do in your car on your way to work. Number 1 on my list that didn't work for my mental health was medication. Now when I say it doesn't work, I mean they don't cure the root of the problem. What they do is block the feeling of having any feeling. So, in a sense, it is like taking Advil when you have a headache. The pain relief is made by blocking the receptors that signals your brain. It doesn't cure what is causing the headache. Now let's say you first start feeling depressed and are considering seeing a doctor or therapist, what happens is that you will fill out a sheet of paper, and based on either your own assessment of (between one to ten) how messed up you feel or the therapist's assessment, I'd say almost everyone is given a prescription. You are then informed that you might not feel some results for weeks. After a couple of weeks, you check in with them again, and they do the same things if you didn't feel like things got better. They will up the dose, and this cycle repeats for months and keeps you for years. Eventually, your so drugged up, it takes extremes to feel happiness or sadness. Medication blocks what makes us, us. That's our spirit. Our spirit connects us to our soul. Without the connection to soul, you lose yourself. I found out after a couple months of self nurturing in nature can change your life and give you that connection your soul needs.

So if you learned anything on my journey, I hope that you learned that people need compassion for themselves. We don't take enough time to process our day and encourage ourselves to strive for better when we really deserve it. We also need to show compassion for the ones we hate because they show us something we can change about ourselves, for the strangers because we don't know what's going on in their lives or who they could be, and for the ones close to us because those are the ones that see the true divinity of your soul. I hope you can incorporate that we are all one under God and he lives in each one of you. So stop the hate across all religion, race, and backgrounds. We are all the same, just old and new souls trying to make it to heaven. How ever you connect with God is up to you.

The power of community is way greater than we may think. The only way the world we all really want and strive for will be here when more people become aware, accept change open- mindedly, and forgive the ones that don't understand you because you and God are the only ones who know you.

I challenge you to start living life to the fullest. Take risks, stop people pleasing, and follow your heart because your heart is the driving force behind your soul's purpose. If you don't know what to do, I suggest taking a walk in the park or that you start journaling because it helps you collect your thoughts and can make for a good book! I'm choosing to be myself, speak my truth and to chase my dreams; you should too.

CPSIA information can be obtained
at www.ICGtesting.com
Printed in the USA
BVHW032256300123
657508BV00008B/47/J